HAPPINESS

HAPPINESS
Todd Solondz

ff

faber and faber

First published in 1998
by Faber and Faber Limited
3 Queen Square London WCIN 3AU

Photoset by Parker Typesetting Service, Leicester
Printed in England by Clays Ltd, St Ives plc

Grateful acknowledgement is made for permission to reprint lines
from the song 'Happiness' by Eytan Mirsky. Copyright © 1998;
Mirsky Mouse Music (BMI). All rights reserved.

A CIP record for this book
is available from the British Library

ISBN 0–571–19792 – 2

2 4 6 8 10 9 7 5 3 1

For my brother Lenny,
who loves his family.

FOREWORD

If you're the kind of person who goes to the movies and actually sits through the credits – and given the fact that you just bought this screenplay, I'd say there's a pretty fair chance that you *are* – you might vaguely remember me as the composer of the title song for Todd Solondz's new film *Happiness*. But that's not why I was asked to write the piece you're reading right now, or at least that's only part of it. I happen to be one of Todd's oldest friends, and he thought it would be nice if someone used this space to write something of a personal nature.

Now the problem with writing something personal is that I don't want to be too revealing and embarrass Todd; he's a very private person. In fact, for a while I thought the only personal thing I could safely tell you about him is that he's the kind of person who doesn't want to reveal anything too personal. Then I remembered something Todd had said in a recent interview. At the height of the initial controversy over *Happiness*, when Universal decided that they no longer wanted their affiliate, October Films, to release Todd's movie, he was asked if that depressed him. No, he answered, 'There are so many more reasons to be depressed.' That casual response perfectly captured his personality – of course he was depressed, but not about that! – and I realized that here, in this part of him that he himself had exposed, was my hook.

You see, people might assume that when someone meets the kind of success Todd has met, when someone is greeted with the kind of acclaim Todd has been greeted with, when someone has reached the lofty heights Todd has reached in his profession, that someone would not be depressed. And that might or might not generally be the case. But I am here to tell you this: success has not spoiled Todd Solondz; he is just as depressed as ever . . . if not more so. And I think that this is a very important thing.

First of all, it clearly affects his choice of subject matter. I'm sure anyone devoted enough to Todd's work to buy this screenplay knows that *Happiness* is no walk in the park. Or rather, it's the kind of walk in the park in which you're likely to see someone pull out a machine-gun and kill everyone in sight. And I bring this up in reference to one of Todd's pet peeves: the 'life-affirming' film. You see, Todd recently related to me the saga of a paralysed man, a quadraplegic who could move only his left eyelid. The man had written a book by blinking as an assistant recited the alphabet. The project took every ounce of his remaining strength to complete, and two days before it was published the author died. The book was praised by reviewers as 'life-affirming'. Now why, Todd wanted to know, was the quality of being 'life-affirming' regarded as an end in itself, something to be praised? I explained that I thought that most people who reviewed books for a living were in fact alive, and that being in that state, they had a bias in favour of life and wanted to see it affirmed. They had chosen to live and basically wanted to be reassured about the wisdom of their choice. (Of course, if life were really so great, it wouldn't need to be affirmed all the time, now would it?)

The flip side to this, of course, is that many people who would be receptive to films that focus on the negative aspects of life – let's not call them 'life-negating' films – have already killed themselves and can't really be counted on as an audience. Thankfully, though, there seem to be enough of them still out there to keep up a steady demand for Todd's films and, I think, to provide each other with a strangely reassuring group bonding experience. Todd himself recently addressed this topic at a symposium at the New School. Asked why he made his last film, *Welcome to the Dollhouse*, he explained that there were many people who had had experiences similar to that of the film's main character, Dawn Wiener, and he wanted them to know they were not alone. Later, though, in private, he said, 'But they *are* alone; they'll always be alone.' And both these feelings contribute to Todd's work; even as he depresses us with the notion that, as in Bill Maplewood's words, 'We're *all* alone', we don't feel so bad, because we're alone together with him, a true kindred spirit.

But I think for Todd the effects of depression go beyond subject matter and in a funny way guide the course of his career. Much could be and probably has been made of the fact that Todd has resisted the siren call of Hollywood, where I'm sure he could command some ungodly salary for directing the big-screen adaptation of some inane and best-forgotten sixties sitcom. But no one has explained that this is because he's so depressed. His outlook on life is so thoroughly negative that he cannot be lured by the things that would ensnare the rest of us: mansions, swimming-pools, glamorous parties, nights on the town with beautiful starlets . . . why pursue them when they only provide the false illusion of happiness? Why bother, when you're bound to be as miserable as you ever were? There really isn't much point. Now personally I am not one who subscribes to this philosophy; I still cling to the vain hope that this or that thing will make my life better. In fact, many were the times over the course of the fifteen years I've known Todd that I tried to interest him in collaborating on the kind of mind-numbing projects that would have made us the second coming of the Zucker brothers. Try as I might, though, my efforts always ended in failure, as the force of Todd's depression gave him the strength to defeat temptation.

Interestingly enough, Todd's point of view is seconded by experts in the field of psychology. I happened to read an article in the last couple of years in the *New York Times* in which the 'happiness' level of a wide range of individuals was studied. The article explained that a generally unhappy person, were he to win the lottery, would perhaps experience a short period of increased happiness, but that within about a year he would return to his formerly unhappy state. Conversely, a generally happy person could basically lose his whole family in a terrible accident and eventually return to his formerly happy state. I think this whole analysis could be tied in fairly well to the film *Happiness*, except for the fact that there's not a single generally happy person in the movie.

Now I hope it doesn't seem like I'm glorifying depression here, engaging in some perverse form of 'bleak chic'. I'm not; and I'm not saying that only depressed people produce great art. Maybe tomorrow Todd will wake up with a total attitude change and start writing sunny romantic comedies, and good for him if he does. But I keep thinking back to 1983, my first year at film school, the year I first met Todd. At the time, neither of us dreamed we even had a chance to attain international success in writing and directing. And I was right; I had no chance! But Todd *did* succeed, beyond all his wildest dreams, first with the rightfully acclaimed *Welcome to the Dollhouse,* and now with his amazing new film, *Happiness.* And to think that through it all he's maintained the same gloomy outlook on life, that he's still just as likely to call and say, 'I'm so depressed', you just have to shake your head in admiration at the purity and beauty of it all.

Eytan Mirsky

Happiness was first shown at the Cannes Film Festival in May 1998.

Writer/Director	Todd Solondz
Producers	Ted Hope, Christine Vachon
Executive Producers	David Linde, James Schamus
Line Producer	Pamela Koffler
Editor	Alan Oxman
Director of Photography	Maryse Alberti
Production Design	Therese Dépréz
Costume Designer	Kathryn Nixon
Music Supervisor	Susan Jacobs
Music	Robbie Kondor
Casting	Ann Goulder

A Good Machine/Killer Films production.

CAST
(in order of appearance)

JOY JORDAN	Jane Adams
ANDY KORNBLUTH	Jon Lovitz
ALLEN	Philip Seymour Hoffman
BILL MAPLEWOOD	Dylan Baker
HELEN JORDAN	Lara Flynn Boyle
TIMMY MAPLEWOOD	Justin Elvin
TRISH MAPLEWOOD	Cynthia Stevenson
CHLOE MAPLEWOOD	Lila Glantzman-Leib
KOOKI	Henry from Animals for Advertising
PSYCHIATRIST	Gerry Becker
BILLY MAPLEWOOD	Rufus Read
MONA JORDAN	Louise Lasser
LENNY JORDAN	Ben Gazzara

Happiness

1 Joy and Andy on their last date.

INT. RESTAURANT – NIGHT

Pretty, thirtyish Joy Jordan and teary-eyed Andy Kornbluth sit opposite each other. He is trying to resist bursting into tears as they finish dessert.

                    JOY
Andy? . . . Are you okay?

                    ANDY
Yeah. Sure. I'm fine.

                    JOY
Good. Well. I had a really nice time.

                    ANDY
Yeah. Me too.

                    JOY
Of course, you know I've always had a really nice time with you.

                    ANDY
Same here.

                    JOY
But . . .

                    ANDY
Yeah.

                    JOY
You understand.

                    ANDY
Uh-huh.

                    JOY
Well. The food here was excellent – I'm gonna recommend it to my sisters! How many stars did it get?

ANDY

Three and a half.

And the dam cracks wide open. He bawls. A pause. He blows his nose.

JOY

Do you feel better now?

Andy nods.

JOY

Me too.

ANDY

Sorry.

JOY

It's really good we had this talk.

ANDY

Yeah.

JOY

Before things went too far . . . You know, got too serious.

ANDY

Oh.

(*a beat*)

Are you sure?

JOY

Oh, yes.

Pause.

ANDY

Is it someone else?

JOY

No, it's just you.

Pause.

ANDY

I want to show you something I got you.

JOY

For me?

ANDY
(*hands her a gift*)
Yeah . . . Open it up.

JOY
(*discovers a pewter ashtray*)
Oh, but, Andy. This is . . . oh, this is beautiful!

ANDY
Thanks. It's a Gainsevoort reproduction. Boston, late 1880s. I sent away for it just after we had our . . . first date.

JOY
Oh, I just love it. It's . . . It's a collector's item.

ANDY
Yeah, it is pretty special.

JOY
It almost makes me want to learn how to smoke!

They laugh.

ANDY
Look at the back.

JOY
(*examines more closely*)
Ooh.

ANDY
That's a forty-carat gold-plated inlaid base.

JOY
Oh, Andy. Thank you. This really means something to me. I'll always treasure it . . . as a token . . .

ANDY
No, you won't.
(*retrieves his gift; a sudden shift in emotion*)
'Cause this is for the girl who loves me. The girl who cares about me, for who I am, not what I look like. I just wanted you to know

5

what you'd be missing. You think I don't appreciate art. You think I don't understand fashion. You think I'm not hip. You think I'm pathetic, a nerd, a lard-ass fatso. You think I'm shit. Well, you're wrong. 'Cause I'm champagne. And you're shit. And till the day you die, you, not me, will always be shit.

FADE TO BLACK.

A TITLE CARD READS: HAPPINESS

CUT TO:

INT. BILL'S OFFICE – DAY

Allen talks to his psychiatrist, Bill Maplewood.

> ALLEN
> . . . I dunno, but whenever I see her I just want to . . . you know
> . . . I want to undress her, I want to tie her up and pump her
> pump pump pump till she screams bloody murder. And then I
> want to flip her ass over and pump her even more and so hard
> that my dick shoots right through her and that my come squirts
> out of her mouth . . . Not that I could ever actually . . . do that
> . . . See, if she only knew how I felt, how deep down I really
> cared for her, respected her, she would love me back. Maybe.
> Oh . . . But she doesn't even know I exist. I mean, she knows I
> exist – we are neighbours, we smile politely at each other . . .
> But I don't know how I could ever begin to really talk to her, I
> mean what can I talk about? I have nothing to talk about. I'm
> boring. I know. I've been told before, so don't tell me it's not
> true. 'Cause it's a fact. I bore people. People look at me and they
> get bored. People listen to me and they zone out, bored . . .
> Who is that boring person? they think, I have never before met
> anyone so boring. And for her to see how boring I am . . .

Allen's voice fades out. Bill's voice fades in.

> BILL
> (*voice-over*)
> . . . gallon of skim milk . . . a dozen eggs . . . one of those
> disposable cameras for the weekend . . . stop at the 7–11 on

the way home . . . pick up the dry-cleaning . . . check Billy's homework . . . call Mrs Mitchell about her appointment on Tuesday . . . get the dog cleaned . . .

Bill dozes off, Allen's voice wakes him up.

ALLEN
. . . but you know what I'm going to do? When I see her next time, as soon as I see her, I'm just going to tell her . . . tell her I, that I . . . find her . . . attractive.

EXT. ALLEN AND HELEN'S APARTMENT COMPLEX – EVENING

Helen Jordan parks, gets out of her car, walks towards the apartment building entrance.

INT. APARTMENT COMPLEX LOBBY – EVENING

Helen walks through the lobby towards the elevator and waits beside Allen.

DOORMAN
Good evening, Ms Jordan.

Helen smiles and nods.

Allen mumbles something. Helen is oblivious.

ALLEN
How's it going?

HELEN
Okay.

The elevator arrives.

INT. ELEVATOR – EVENING

Allen and Helen ride in silence up to their floor.

INT. HALLWAY – EVENING

Allen and Helen emerge from the elevator.

2 Allen and Helen wait for the elevator.

ALLEN

See ya.

HELEN

Yeah.

And they walk their separate ways.

INT. ALLEN'S BATHROOM – EVENING

Allen takes a shower.

INT. ALLEN'S APARTMENT – EVENING

Allen starts flipping randomly through the phone book. He turns to a bookmarked page.

ALLEN
(*mumbling*)
I'm going to fuck you so hard . . . you'll be coming out of your ears . . . Fuck you . . .

He dials a number from the book. A man picks up.

MAN
(*voice-over*)

Yeah?

Allen hangs up.

ALLEN
I'll fuck you . . . I'll fuck you . . . really hard . . . So hard you won't even . . .

He dials another number.

ALLEN

Hello, is this Claire?

WOMAN
(*voice-over*)

Who is this?

Allen hangs up, knocks over some furniture.

INT. MAPLEWOOD FOYER – DAY

A maid scrubs the floor as cute little Timmy Maplewood, dressed in a Robocop-like costume, runs by.

INT. MAPLEWOOD KITCHEN – DAY

Joy sits chatting in the kitchen with her sister Trish Maplewood, who is fixing a little snack. Trish's baby Chloe sits with a pacifier in a high chair. Kooki the dog lies on the floor in the background.

Timmy suddenly bursts into the room, firing a toy laser gun.

> TIMMY
> *(aiming his gun at Joy)*
> Die, Aunt Joy! Die!

> TRISH
> Timmy!

She tries to go after him, but he has already run off.

> JOY
> It's okay, Trish. He's just going through a phase. Leave him alone.

> TRISH
> I know, but . . .

> JOY
> *(trying to make light)*
> It's okay. I'm strong enough.

> TRISH
> I blame it on cartoons. They are so full of violence. And what's with the people that are making cartoons? That's what you have to –
> *(suddenly realizes Joy is in tears)*
> Joy, Joy. What's the matter?

> JOY
> I don't know what it is, but I feel there's so much hostility directed at me.

TRISH

Did another guy dump you?

JOY

No! I . . . oh, I feel terrible.

TRISH

Aww. Timmy didn't mean it.

JOY

No, I know . . . I know . . . I'm sorry. I – I'm overworked.
That's all.

TRISH

It's okay. Because now maybe you'll listen to me.

JOY

What?

A weighty pause.

TRISH

You've got to eat red meat.

JOY

Oh, Trish . . .

TRISH

Oh, I knew how you'd react, but I'm telling you, it's true. I've
been watching you and, well . . . My doctor says just once a
month . . .

JOY

I know . . .

TRISH

Really. It's the best thing for the skin. It'll clear it all up.

JOY

What's wrong with my skin?

TRISH

Well, it's fine now, but in another few years . . . Please, Joy.
You know I'm just speaking for your own good.

JOY

Oh, I know. I know. Thanks.

A tender moment: Trish and Joy hold hands.

JOY

I'm so happy.

TRISH

Are you really?

JOY

Being around you and the kids . . . Kooki . . .

TRISH

Oh . . . And I'm so happy you're happy. 'Cause all this time
I've been thinking you were so miserable.

JOY

Oh, Trish! That's too funny, when I couldn't be happier.

TRISH

It's just, what with your music career never really . . .

JOY

Oh, my career's fine!

TRISH

Oh, I know, it will be! I just know it! And then you'll move
out of Mom and Dad's . . .

JOY

Real soon!

TRISH

And you'll meet Mr Right!

JOY

Oh, I will. Already I feel I'm off to a fresh start!

TRISH

That's right. Just because you've hit thirty doesn't mean you
can't be fresh any more.

Pause.

You know, Joy, I've never told you this before, but now that we're older, and I feel so bonded to you, well . . . the truth is – oh, I know this is going to sound horrible, but I just feel I have to be fully open with you, get beyond all the old barriers, the sibling nonsense – well, the truth is I always thought you would never amount to much. That you'd end up alone, without a career or anything. Really, it's what we all thought. Mom, Dad, Helen . . . everyone . . . I'd always prayed we'd all be wrong, but you had always seemed so . . . doomed to failure. But now I see that's not true. There's a glimmer of hope for you after all. Oh, I know I'm repeating myself, but, oh . . .

> (*tears well up*)

I'm just really happy for you . . .

EXT. PARK – DAY

It is sunny and warm. Couples straight and gay walk hand in hand, families picnic, beautiful people sunbathe together.

Bill observes the pleasant tranquillity from atop a hill. Suddenly he pulls out a machine-gun and starts shooting at everyone.

Bloodshed everywhere. Then silence.

> VOICE
> And how is this different?

INT. PSYCHIATRIST'S OFFICE – DAY

Bill sits opposite his Psychiatrist, to whom the voice belongs.

> BILL
> I don't kill myself at the end.

> PSYCHIATRIST
> So you see this as something positive?

> BILL
> Gee, I don't know.

> PSYCHIATRIST
> How do you feel at the end?

13

                              BILL

Much better. I wake up happy, feeling good. But then I get
very depressed because I'm living in reality.

                          PSYCHIATRIST

And what about your family?

                              BILL

Trish is good to me.

                          PSYCHIATRIST

But still no sex?

                              BILL

No, but she's not too interested either. So really there's no
problem there when you think about it, on a certain level.

INT. BILL'S CAR – DAY

Bill is driving along, listening to light classical music.

EXT. MINI-MALL – DAY

Bill pulls into the lot. He walks into a 7–11.

INT. 7–11 – DAY

Bill picks up a copy of Kool, *a hip magazine for pre-teen boys.*

EXT. MINI-MALL – DAY

Bill gets into the back seat of his car and sets to masturbating.

*Shoppers walk by with shopping carts, little children, oblivious to the
activity inside Bill's car.*

INT. MAPLEWOOD KITCHEN – EVENING

*Bill comes home as Trish finishes preparing dinner. He gives her a peck
on the cheek.*

                              BILL

Hey.

TRISH

So how was work today, hon?

BILL

Oh, fine.

Billy enters from the TV room, opens the refrigerator, pulls out a glass of soda. He looks dejected.

BILL

Hey, Billy! What's going on?

BILLY

Nothing.

TRISH

He's
            (*making quotation marks with her fingers*)
'depressed'.

BILL

Well, is anything the matter?

BILLY

I don't wanna talk about it.

And he returns to the TV room.

TRISH

Ignore him. He's just doing it for attention. He thinks you'll be impressed. As if. So anyway . . . Joy came by today.

BILL

How's she doing?

TRISH

Oh, God, I dunno, and frankly . . . I'm concerned. I mean, she's not like me. She doesn't 'have it all'. She pretends to be happy, but I can see right through her: she's miserable.

BILL

Why do you think that is?

TRISH

To be frank, I think she's lazy. She's not a go-getter, like me or Helen. And she's so picky. I gave Damien Ross her phone number, for what it's worth, and Joy sounded interested, naturally, but . . . I dunno. I'm afraid to have to say it, but truly it's what I believe: she'll always be alone.

BILL

We're all alone.

TRISH

Oh, Bill. Sometimes I wonder how any of your patients can talk to you!

BILL

Sometimes I wonder if they'll ever stop. I should tape some for you.

TRISH

Oh, Bill would you? Would you really? So that I could listen too?

BILL

No.

TRISH

Oh, come on . . . You're such a tease. You know I wouldn't tell anyone.

BILL

Right. 'Cause you're so secretive.

TRISH

Well, maybe not as secretive as you.

BILL

What secret would you like me to tell you?

Trish puts her arms around Bill.

TRISH
(*whispers coyly*)
Like how come no matter how much you treat me like shit, I can't help loving you even more?

They kiss.

3 '*What secret would you like me to tell you?*'

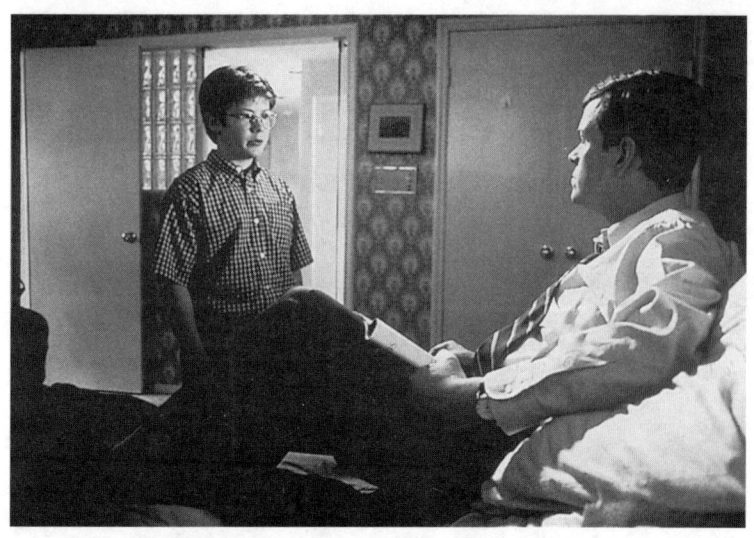

4 Billy seeks some guidance from his father.

INT. BILL AND TRISH'S BEDROOM – LATER

While Trish puts Chloe and Timmy to sleep, Billy comes and sits beside Bill on his bed.

> BILLY

Dad?

> BILL

Yes, Billy?

> BILLY

What does come mean?

> BILL

Come?

> BILLY

You know . . .

> BILL

Well, you know how sometimes your penis gets erect . . .
well, sometimes it gets so excited that a sticky milky
substance shoots out.

BILLY

. . . Dickwad?

BILL

Yes, only come can be used as a verb as well.
            (*a beat*)
Billy?

BILLY

Yeah?

BILL

Have you ever come?

BILLY

Yeah . . .

BILL

Now, Billy, it's all right if you haven't.

BILLY

But, I have . . .

BILL

Billy . . .

BILLY

But everyone else in class has and . . . I want to come, too!

Billy starts crying.

BILL

Aw, now, it's okay, it's okay. Have you tried playing with
yourself?

BILLY

You mean . . .

BILL

With your penis.

BILLY

A little.

BILL

How did it feel?

BILLY

I dunno. I don't know what to do.

BILL

Do you want me to . . . show you?

BILLY

No! No! I'm not normal!

Billy buries his head in Bill's shoulder.

BILL

Aw, Billy. Don't worry. You're normal. You'll come. One day. You'll see.

EXT. CONDOMINIUM COMPLEX – DAY

It is bright and sunny.

LENNY
(*voice-over*)

I'm turning on the dishwasher!

INT. LENNY AND MONA JORDAN'S CONDO – DAY

Mona is lying motionless on top of the bed in her bedroom.

Finally she gets up, shuffles to the bathroom, opens the medicine cabinet.

MONA
(*calling, faux calm*)

Where's my Valium?!

LENNY
(*off-screen*)

What?!

MONA

Nevermind!
(*to herself*)

Fucking asshole.

She has found a good enough Valium substitute. She swallows a couple of pills.

The phone rings.

> MONA
> (*to herself*)

You answer it, bastard.

> LENNY
> (*off-screen*)

Mona . . . It's Trish!

Mona picks up.

> MONA

Hi, Trish!

> TRISH
> (*voice-over*)

Hi, Mom. How are you?

> MONA

Oh, I'm fine. How are you?

> TRISH
> (*voice-over*)

Fine . . .

> MONA

Good.

> TRISH
> (*voice-over*)

Did you watch Leno last night? . . . Mom?

Pause.

> MONA
> (*bursts into tears*)

He's leaving me! Your father's leaving me!

> TRISH
> (*voice-over*)

Mom, what are you talking about?

> MONA

Trish, can you keep this secret? Top secret?

                              TRISH
                            (*voice-over*)
        Yes, yes, of course I can, Mom, but –

                              MONA
        He says . . . he says he doesn't love me any more.

                              TRISH
                            (*voice-over*)
        Mom, I'm sure he doesn't mean it.

                              MONA
        Well, he does fucking mean it! He wants a divorce!

                              TRISH
                            (*voice-over*)
        He said the word divorce?

                              MONA
        What . . . You don't believe me? You talk to him!
                            (*calling*)
        Lenny!

                              LENNY
        Yeah?!

                              MONA
        It's Trish! She wants to talk to you!

INT. TRISH'S KITCHEN – DAY

Trish is holding Chloe while talking on the phone.

                              LENNY
                    (*voice-over; on phone*)
        Yeah, Trish?

                              TRISH
        Is it true what Mom said?

                              LENNY
                            (*voice-over*)
        What?

                              22

TRISH

You want a divorce?

LENNY
(voice-over)

Mona! What are you telling the kids?!

INT. LENNY AND MONA'S CONDO – DAY

The living-room. Lenny is sitting on the couch, talking to Trish on the phone and watching a baseball game on TV.

Mona comes wobbling into the room.

LENNY
(to Trish)

She'll call you back.
(hangs up; to Mona)
Did I use the word divorce?

MONA

You said you didn't want to live with me any more!

LENNY

Answer my question: did I use the word divorce?

MONA

You said you didn't love me any more!

LENNY

Did I use the word divorce?!

MONA

. . . No.

LENNY

Good. I just want that clear. Now sit down now next to me. Come on. Sit down.
(yells)

Sit down!

Mona sits next to him. Pause.

MONA

Lenny . . . Why?

23

5 Lenny and Mona face the baseball game on TV.

LENNY

I dunno. I just want to be alone.

MONA

I can let you be alone more, if that's what you want . . .

LENNY

It's not that: things change . . . People change . . . I want out.

Pause.

MONA

It's Diane.

LENNY

Diane?

MONA

You're in love with Diane Freed.

LENNY

Get outta here.

24

MONA

Well, you're in love with someone. And it's someone
younger, probably.

LENNY

Wrong.

MONA

Lenny, it's okay. I'm not dumb. These things happen. I'll get
over it. I just wish you had done this twenty years ago. Now
I'll have to get another fucking face-lift!

Pause

LENNY

I'm in love with no one.

MONA

No one?

LENNY

No one.

MONA

Okay, then.
(*a beat*)
Schmuck.

EXT. HELEN'S APARTMENT BUILDING – DAY

HELEN
(*voice-over*)
Y'know, people are always putting New Jersey down.

INT. HELEN'S APARTMENT – DAY

*Helen is on the phone. Jamal, a very muscular stud, lifts weights on her
bed.*

HELEN

None of my friends can actually believe I live here. But that's
because they don't get it: I'm living in a state of irony.

INT. JOY'S PLACE – DAY

Joy is on the phone in her kitchen, preparing dinner for two.

JOY

Helen, are you sure you don't wanna come over and have dinner with me?

BACK TO:

Helen rising, looking for some papers.

HELEN

I can't. I'm giving another reading/book-signing at Barnes & Noble, then Jamal is taking me out – although I promised Flavio . . . Uch. I hate Saturday nights. Everybody wants me, Joy, you have no idea.

BACK TO:

JOY

Oh, I know. It's just that I wrote a new song and I thought maybe you'd come over and I'd play it for you.

HELEN
(*voice-over*)

Can you hold a second?

BACK TO:

HELEN
(*clicks the call-waiting button*)

Hello? . . . Oh, Salman! Hold on one second.
(*clicks back to Joy*)

Joy, I'm sorry, but I have to take this, it's London. But I'll talk to you soon, okay? Bye!

BACK TO:

JOY

Bye.

Joy puts away the extra food, prepares to cook a steak for herself.

The phone rings, she answers it.

JOY

Hello?

VOICE

Hi! How are you?

JOY

Is this . . . Damien?

VOICE

Yeah! . . . Uh, so how are you doing?

JOY

Oh, fine! Trish told me you might be calling.

VOICE

Yeah, well . . .

JOY

Oh, I know how weird these things can be, but I've always
had such faith in Trish's judgment that I thought why not. It's
not like I've got some huge social life. I mean, I do have a
social life. It's just not huge.

VOICE

Same here.

JOY

Oh, really? That's so nice to hear. Most people seem so
confident . . .

VOICE

Yeah . . .

JOY

Or, well, you know . . . They're just real jerks . . .

Joy pounds her frozen steak.

VOICE

Yeah . . . uh . . . What are you doing?

JOY

Oh, I'm sorry, I'm just trying to thaw this steak . . . and it's so
hard and . . . I'm sorry.

27

VOICE

Oh, no. No. Don't stop. Not because of me.

JOY

Well, it's just I feel I'm being so rude.

VOICE

No, no. Not at all.

JOY

Thanks.

VOICE

Uhh . . . Are you alone?

JOY

Yeah. I'm all alone. Nobody's listening in. God, you're just like me.

VOICE

Uh . . . What are you wearing?

Split screen now reveals Allen is on the other end of this phone call.

JOY

You mean, when we go out? Well, where do you want to go? I mean, I'm pretty easy to please. I hate getting all dressed up.

VOICE

What are you wearing now?

JOY

Oh, just a pair of jeans. Why?

VOICE

Are they tight?

JOY

Not too tight. Actually they fit pretty well. But why do you . . . ?

VOICE

Not the jeans. Underneath. What are you wearing underneath? Check.

28

JOY
(*starts looking inside her jeans*)
Underneath? Well, but, Damien, underneath is just . . .
(*pauses, suddenly alarmed*)
This isn't Damien . . . is it?

VOICE
Are you all wet? Is your pussy all wet?

Joy hangs up.

INT. ALLEN'S BEDROOM – THAT MOMENT

Allen notices the mess he made on the wallpaper. The stain looks permanent. He covers it up with a postcard. (There are many other postcards already stuck to the wall.)

The doorbell rings.

He rises.

ALLEN
Who is it?

VOICE
It's your neighbour Kristina.

Allen opens the door, sees Kristina She is very big and very overweight.

ALLEN
Hey, what's up?

KRISTINA
Did you hear what happened to Pedro?

ALLEN
Who's Pedro?

KRISTINA
You know, the night doorman?

ALLEN
Oh, yeah. What?

29

KRISTINA

He was found bludgeoned to death in his apartment this
morning.

ALLEN

Uch.

KRISTINA

Yeah. And supposedly his penis was missing.

ALLEN

Uugh.

KRISTINA

Anyway, Carla in #2B, she's collecting money for the funeral,
if you feel like it. Apparently he had no family, no known
friends . . . If I'da known . . . I did always say hi, I think.

ALLEN

Me too. If it's the guy I'm thinking of.

Pause.

KRISTINA

By the way, um, I've got an extra ticket to the play-offs
tonight. Wanna come with me?

ALLEN

Nah. Thanks. I got too much work.

KRISTINA

Well, anyway, I just thought I'd tell you about Pedro.

ALLEN

Thanks.

KRISTINA

See ya.

ALLEN

Yeah.

And he closes the door.

INT. HALLWAY – THAT MOMENT

Kristina stands outside Allen's door and stares at it dejectedly. Finally, tearing up the tickets, she walks back to her apartment.

EXT. JOY'S PLACE – EVENING

Joy is sitting on her bed with her guitar, playing her song, 'Happiness'.

A display of macramé objets d'art adorns the wall.

JOY
(singing)

It seems the things I've wanted in my life
I've never had.
And so it's no surprise
that living only leaves me sad.

Happiness, where are you?
I've searched so long for you.
Happiness, what are you?
I haven't got a clue.
Happiness, why do you have to
stay so far away from me?

When I'm in despair
and life has turned into a mess
I know that I don't dare
to end my search for happiness.
Happiness, where are you?
I –

The phone rings. She answers it.

JOY

Hello?

INT. ANDY'S PLACE – EVENING

A plastic 'World of Pewter' bag is untied and pulled off Andy's dead head. The pewter ashtray is removed from his rigid hand. Policemen, a Coroner et al. busy themselves while Andy's body is removed. Detective Berman holds Andy's suicide note in a baggie in his hand.

6 Joy sings 'Happiness'.

BERMAN
(*on the phone*)

Hello. This is Detective Berman from the County Police Department. I'd like to speak to a Ms Joy Jordan?

JOY
(*voice-over*)

This is she.

BERMAN

I'm sorry to disturb you, Ms Jordan, but I'm afraid I have some bad news for you . . .

EXT. OFFICE BUILDING COMPLEX – DAY

A bright, cheerful day.

BERMAN
(*voice-over*)

. . . It's regarding an acquaintance of yours, an Andrew Kornbluth . . .

INT. JOY'S OFFICE – DAY

Joy looks over at a corner desk where a woman is working the phones, and starts crying. Her neighbour Nancy, hearing the sniffling, pauses in the midst of her work.

NANCY

Joy, are you okay?

JOY

Yeah . . . sure . . . I'm fine.

NANCY

What's the matter?

JOY

Andy's dead!

NANCY

Andy . . . ?

JOY

Yes!

Pause.

NANCY

Who's Andy?

JOY

You know, the guy who used to work right over there in that corner?

NANCY

You mean where Pam is sitting?

JOY

Yes!

NANCY

Was he kind of tall and a little hunched?

JOY

No, he was . . . well . . . a little shortish, a little squarish . . .

NANCY

Joy. I'm not sure. Did he work here long?

JOY

Oh, a year, maybe a little over . . .

Nancy calls across to another neighbour, Kay.

NANCY

Kay, do you remember a guy named Andy who used to work here over where Pam is now?

KAY

No. Why? What happened?

NANCY

He died.

KAY

Huh. Which one was he?

34

I'm not sure. Maybe Tom knows. Tom?

Co-worker Tom, who has been listening in, swivels over from the other side.

TOM

Sorry, Nancy, I don't. I mean, I do vaguely remember some guy who worked over there – I think . . . but I'm not really sure.

KAY

How did he die?

NANCY

Yeah, Joy, how did he die?

Joy's phone rings. She picks up.

JOY

Sales, may I help you?

VOICE

Is this Joy Jordan?

JOY

Yes.

VOICE

This is Andy's mother.
            (*a beat*)
I hope you fucking rot in hell.

The voice hangs up.

TOM

Joy. Was he kind of Latino-looking and a little acne-scarred?

NANCY

Oh, yeah, you know, like what's his name . . . you know . . . the actor . . .

JOY
(*a beat*)

Yeah. Sure. That was him.

TOM

That's him . . . that's him . . . that actor!

NANCY

What actor?

TOM

Oh, it has A in it. It's . . . you know . . . something . . .
something . . . something.

NANCY

Oh yeah. I can picture his face but I can't think of what he's
been in.

TOM

Yeah . . . J something.

KAY

J . . . J . . . If I go through the alphabet I can usually figure
out . . .

*Nancy, Kay and Tom continue discussing and disputing Andy's
identity.*

INT. RESTAURANT – DAY

*Helen and Trish sit together next to where Joy and Andy had sat
earlier.*

HELEN
(*picking at her food*)
Uch. I don't know why I suggested this place. Joy
recommended it . . .

TRISH

Well, at least we're together. I never get to see you, you're so
busy.

HELEN

You're so busy.

TRISH

No, you are . . .

HELEN

No, you are.

TRISH

No, you are.

HELEN

Well, I guess I am.

TRISH

Me too.

HELEN

In fact, if I have to do one more interview . . .

TRISH

I guess it's hard, all this success.

HELEN

It's just I'm so tired of . . . of being admired all the time. I mean all these men . . . they're beautiful, artistic minds, great sex, the whole package . . . but hollow, you know what I mean? I feel nobody's honest with me. Nobody wants me for me.

TRISH

They're not family.

HELEN

Oh, Trish. I wish I had your life – husband, kids, car pool . . .

TRISH

Well, I may 'have it all', but you know sometimes I wonder what my life might have been like if I'd actually tried to write a novel.

HELEN

I'm sure it would have been good.

TRISH

Maybe I will write one.

HELEN

You should . . . Just try . . .

Pause.

TRISH

No, I don't need that kind of success.

HELEN

Listen to us. We who have everything while Joy . . . What does she have?

TRISH

You're so right. And she's just getting older.

HELEN

Last night she called while I was in bed with Huraki – I think – and she was in tears. She told me she'd quit her job . . .

TRISH

Oh, but . . . but that's her lifeline!

HELEN

She said she wanted to 'change' her life. Do 'good', work with the poor, the needy . . .

TRISH

I don't get it.

HELEN

Don't even try. She doesn't understand she already *is* good. She doesn't need to *do* good.

TRISH

And what about her music career?

HELEN

I don't know, but don't hold your breath. Anyway, listen. This is all top secret. She doesn't want anyone to know.

TRISH

Oh.
(*a beat*)
But she told you.

HELEN

She felt she could trust me.

TRISH

'Cause I always thought I was someone that she could confide in.

A busboy comes by, refills their water glasses, leaves.

TRISH

Did you speak to Mom?

HELEN

You mean about the split-up?

TRISH

Oh. I – I thought that was all top secret.

HELEN

Just for Joy. Sensitive Joy. Everyone else knows.

TRISH

Oh.

A waiter comes by.

WAITER

Can I get you ladies anything else? Coffee . . . Dessert?

HELEN

Oh, no, just the check.

The waiter leaves the check, clears the plates, goes off. Trish picks up the check, looks at it.

HELEN

Thanks for lunch. I really enjoyed this.

EXT. ESL SCHOOL – DAY

Picketers march along the sidewalk. Joy approaches, then hesitates.

PICKETERS
(*chanting*)
Benefits! Benefits! We want benefits!

JOY

You know, there are some people in real need in there.

Fucking management is in there!

JOY

But what about the refugees?

PICKETER 2

What about our benefits?!

JOY

I'm sorry. I think you're all making a terrible mistake.

PICKETER 1

Fucking scab!

PICKETERS
(*in unison*)

Scab! Scab! Scab!

As she crosses the picket line they throw rotten vegetables at her. She runs inside.

INT. ESL SCHOOLTEACHERS' LOUNGE – DAY

The atmosphere is casual, business-as-usual, if not quite festive.

Joy wanders her way over to the window, looks out. The shouts of protest from outside can still be heard.

Rhonda, a teacher, comes over and looks out the window, too.

RHONDA

It's so sad. I mean, it's pathetic. Such losers. Really, I feel sorry for them.

There is a slight commotion across the room. Teacher 1 is upset, crying a little. Teacher 2 comforts her.

TEACHER 2

What is it? What happened?

TEACHER 1

. . . They called me a scab.

TEACHER 2

You are not a scab. You're a strike-breaker.

The bell rings.

RHONDA
(to Joy)

Good luck!

INT. CLASSROOM – DAY

Joy enters. The students do not have welcoming faces.

JOY

Good morning. My name is Joy Jordan.

She writes her name on the blackboard.

JOY

I am your new teacher. Now.

Joy is about to do roll-call when:

STUDENT 1

You are scab.

STUDENT 2

Where Marsha?

JOY

Marsha? Well, Marsha . . . er . . .

STUDENT 3

We want Marsha.

The students start chanting, 'We want Marsha!' One student, however, does not join in. He shouts at his classmates:

VLAD

Quiet!

They listen to him.

VLAD
(to Joy)

Please.

JOY

. . . I am not a scab. I am a strike-breaker.

EXT. PARK — DAY

A little league game is in progress. Billy hits the ball, makes it to first.

> BILL
> Go, Billy! All right! Good job!

Bill suddenly notices eleven-year-old Johnny Grasso now at bat. He walks over, as if in a trance, towards the fence behind the umpire. He can't take his eyes off him.

Johnny strikes out. His father, Joe Grasso, the team's coach, curses.

INT. FAST FOOD RESTAURANT — DAY

While Billy and Johnny play video games, Bill and Joe eat at a table.

> JOE
> Bill, I dunno. Maybe I should talk to you. You're supposed to be a specialist in these things, aren't you?

> BILL
> Well, I don't know. That depends . . .

> JOE
> Look, my son's a fag. I'm not blind to these things.

> BILL
> How come you're so sure he's . . . gay?

> JOE
> What, are you kidding?

> BILL
> Well, it's just sometimes . . . appearances can be deceiving. And besides. Even if you're right. There's not much you can do, is there?

Pause.

> JOE
> What do you think would happen if I got him a professional . . . you know . . .

> BILL
> A professional . . .?

42

JOE

Hooker. You know, the kind that can teach things . . . first-timers, you know . . . break him in . . .

BILL

But, Joe, he's eleven.

JOE

Yeah you're right, you're right. It's too late. He is . . . what he is. Forget I said anything.

Billy and Johnny approach.

BILLY

Dad, can Johnny sleep over tonight?

BILL

Well, that's up to Joe here.

JOHNNY

Daddy, may I please sleep over Billy's tonight?

JOE
(*pause*)

Sure. Sure. Whatever.

7 Johnny asks permission to sleep over at Billy's

Yeah!!!

Johnny and Billy hold each other as they jump for joy.

> JOE
> (*to himself*)

Like girls.

INT. MAPLEWOOD KITCHEN – NIGHT

Bill is preparing hot-fudge sundaes. He mixes some powdered drugs into the fudge before pouring it on to the ice-cream.

INT. MAPLEWOOD TV ROOM – NIGHT

Bill brings in a tray loaded with bowls of sundaes.

> BILL

Come and get it!

> TRISH

Oh, Bill. You shouldn't have.

> BILL

Here, take. You only live once.

Everyone grabs a bowl, except Johnny.

Here, Johnny.

> JOHNNY

No, thank you, Dr Maplewood.

> BILL

Aren't you having?

> BILLY

Johnny hates chocolate fudge.

> BILL

Well, is there something you'd like instead?

> JOHNNY

No, thank you.

                              BILL
What about to drink?

                             TRISH
Oh, leave him alone, honey. He's fine.

                              BILL
No, but there must be something . . .

                            JOHNNY
Do you have any grape Hi C?

                              BILL
Do we, Trish?

                             TRISH
I'm afraid not.

                              BILL
I'll go pick some up.

                             TRISH
Bill, don't be silly. He doesn't need anything. It's late.

                            JOHNNY
Do you have any tuna salad?

                              BILL
Would you like a sandwich?

                            JOHNNY
Yes, please.

                              BILL
Coming right up!

INT. MAPLEWOOD KITCHEN – NIGHT

Bill hastily fixes a tuna sandwich, spiking it with gobs of his powder.

Trish and Timmy appear in the background.

                             TRISH
We're going to bed, hon. Little Timmy can hardly keep his
eyes open. Come on, Timmy.
                    (*calls to Billy and Johnny*)

                               45

You boys don't stay up too late!

INT. MAPLEWOOD TV ROOM – NIGHT

Bill brings the sandwich in to Johnny. He finds Billy already fallen asleep.

> BILL
> Here we are! Hey, what happened to Billy?

> JOHNNY
> I don't know. I guess he just conked out.

> BILL
> Bedtime for Billy.

INT. MAPLEWOOD HOUSE UPSTAIRS – NIGHT

Bill carries Billy upstairs and tucks him in. He checks on the baby and then on Trish.

INT. MAPLEWOOD TV ROOM – NIGHT

Bill returns to find Johnny glued to the TV. He hasn't even touched the tuna sandwich.

> BILL
> Aren't you going to eat the sandwich?

> JOHNNY
> In a minute.

> BILL
> Take your time.

Bill waits.

> BILL
> Is your game almost over?

> JOHNNY
> This is the bonus round.

> BILL
> Would you like some cereal . . . maybe a hot dog?

JOHNNY

No, thank you.
                    (*pause*)
Dr Maplewood, would it be all right if I ate this tomorrow?

BILL
                (*not losing his self-control*)
Well, sure, but I don't know if it's gonna taste any good
tomorrow.

*Johnny examines the sandwich. He turns back to the TV. Just when all
seems lost, however, he takes a bite.*

BILL

How is it?

JOHNNY

Actually, it's really good.

Fade to black.

EXT. MAPLEWOOD HOME – MORNING

A little boy bicycles by. Other little children play ball off-screen.

INT. BILL AND TRISH'S BEDROOM – MORNING

Trish snuggles in bed next to Bill.

TRISH

Oh, honey. I feel so good now.

BILL

Me too.

TRISH

I don't think I've slept this well in so long.

BILL

Me neither.

TRISH

It's weird. I feel as if we . . . Bill, did we? Did you . . . Did
I . . .?

BILL

Yes.

Pause.

TRISH

I don't remember . . .

BILL

It's all right. It doesn't matter.

Pause.

TRISH

It matters.

BILL

Forget about it.

TRISH

Okay.
(*a beat*)
It's funny, 'cause I remember I was dreaming and you were there . . . and Billy . . . and Timmy and Chloe . . . and Johnny Grasso . . .

BILL

Oh?

TRISH

I can't really remember anything more, except . . . I don't know. Oh, Bill. Please don't get mad at me, I know you hate it when I ask, but . . . Do you still . . .?

BILL

Oh.

TRISH

Oh.

Pause.

BILL

Yes. Very very much.

                    TRISH

Oh, Bill, and I do too! I'm sorry I need to keep being
reminded, it's just . . .

                    BILL

I know.

                    TRISH

And we haven't been . . .

                    BILL

I know. And it's my fault.

                    TRISH

No, it's my fault.

                    BILL

Trish, I –

                    TRISH

I know.

                    BILL

No, I . . . I –

INT. MAPLEWOOD KITCHEN – DAY

*Johnny sits at the table with the funnies. Bill is sipping coffee, reading
the paper.*

Timmy runs by with his laser gun, shouting:

                    TIMMY

DIE! DIE! DIE! DIE!

                    BILL

Where's Billy?

                    JOHNNY

Watching TV.

                    BILL

How come you two aren't playing together?

                    JOHNNY

I don't know. Billy just said he didn't feel like it.

                    49

(a beat)

Dr Maplewood?

BILL

Yes?

JOHNNY

Can you drive me home now?

BILL

Well, sure, but . . . aren't you having a good time?

JOHNNY

I'm not feeling very well.

BILL

What's the matter?

JOHNNY

I don't know.

He throws up on the funnies.

BILL

Oh . . . er . . . all right. I'll take you home.

INT. BILL'S CAR – DAY

Bill is driving Johnny home.

JOHNNY

Dr Maplewood?

BILL

Yes, Johnny?

JOHNNY

I'm sorry I threw up.

BILL

Don't worry about it.

JOHNNY

'Cause I really had a good time.

BILL

Good. Billy did too. We all did.

8 Bill drives Johnny home.

Bill puts his arm around him affectionately. Johnny, very sleepy, leans in close against him.

JOHNNY

Dr Maplewood?

BILL

Yes, Johnny?

JOHNNY

You're so cool.

And he falls asleep, his head sinking into Bill's lap.

INT. MAPLEWOOD TV ROOM – LATER

Billy sits beside Bill on the couch.

BILLY

Dad?

BILL

Yes, Billy?

                                BILLY
      I was kind of wondering.

                                BILL
      Yes?

Pause.

                                BILLY
      Nothing.

Pause.

                                BILL
      Did you have fun with Johnny?

                                BILLY
      Yeah . . . It was okay. He's a little girlish, though.

                                BILL
      Oh. Yeah.

Pause.

                                BILLY
      Dad, do you know how many inches your penis is?

Pause.

                                BILL
      I never measured.

                                BILLY
      'Cause Ronald Farber said his penis is eleven inches long. Do
      you think that's possible?

                                BILL
      What Ronald Farber doesn't know is that it's not length that
      matters; it's width.

Pause.

                                BILLY
      Why?

                                BILL
      Things get a little more . . . intense.

                                52

Pause.

> BILLY

What do you mean . . . intense?

Pause.

> BILL

Have you been . . . practising?

> BILLY

. . . Yeah. But it's no use. Nothing comes.

> BILL

You have to be patient. Your friend Ronald Farber, I can assure you, is full of crap.

> BILLY

Yeah. I bet yours is a lot wider and longer.

Pause.

> BILL

Do you want me to measure?

> BILLY

Nah, that's okay.

Billy smiles.

INT. BOCA RATON REAL ESTATE OFFICE – DAY

Mona is sitting in the waiting-room when Ann Chambeau, a young and comely broker, appears.

> ANN

Hi. Ann Chambeau.

> MONA

Oh. Mona Jordan.

> ANN

Wonderful.
> (*shakes hands with Mona*)
Come this way. I'm sorry to have kept you waiting so long.

Ann escorts Mona to her desk.

53

9 Ann Chambeau, Mona's Florida real estate broker.

ANN

Can I get you some coffee or tea?

MONA

No, thanks.

They sit down.

ANN

Okay. Now then. How can I help you?

MONA

Oh . . . You said that there might be something available over
in Elysian Fields?

ANN

Well, actually we have several places we can see there. But
first I need to get a bit of information from you.
              (*starts typing into her computer*)
Are you looking for a one, two or three-bedroom?

MONA

Three.

ANN

Wonderful. Is this then for you and your husband?

MONA

No.

ANN

Just yourself then?

MONA

Yes.

ANN

No children?

MONA

All my children are grown.

ANN

No pets?

MONA

No.

ANN

So really then just you alone all by yourself?

MONA

Yes.

ANN

Wonderful.

Ann resumes interfacing with the computer.

Suddenly Mona starts crying. Ann looks up from her terminal.

ANN

Mrs Jordan? Is something the matter?

Mona nods yes and no. Finally:

MONA

My husband is leaving me.

ANN

Oh, I'm so sorry.

Ann reaches her hand out in a vague display of support and affection.

ANN

You know, we have a lot of divorcées in Phase IV. Would you like to see something there, perhaps a bit smaller?

MONA

Who said I was getting divorced?

EXT. LUXURY CONDO VILLAGE – DAY

Ann drives Mona through this scenic luxury community. They pause at a security checkpoint before looking for a spot in the parking lot.

ANN
(*voice-over*)

What you need is a fresh start.

MONA
(*voice-over*)

Yes, that's what I'm looking for.

INT. ANN'S CAR – DAY

Mona turns to Ann as she pulls into a spot.

> ANN
>
> You know, I'm a divorcée.

> MONA
>
> Oh?

> ANN
>
> And I live in Phase IV.

> MONA
>
> I am so sorry.

> ANN
>
> Mrs Jordan?

> MONA
>
> Mona.

> ANN
>
> Mona. That's a beautiful name.

> MONA
>
> Er . . . thank you.

> ANN
>
> How long were you married?

> MONA
>
> Forty years.

Pause.

> ANN
>
> You know, Mona, I think we have a lot in common. Probably
> more than you realize. See, I know what you're going through.
> I've been there. But I'd like to share a little secret with you:
> Divorce was the best thing that ever happened to me.

Ann reaches out and this time touches Mona, gives her a squeeze.

> ANN
>
> Really.

INT. LUXURY CONDO LOBBY – DAY

Ann and Mona walk across the expensively decorated space. It is empty except for an old lady with a walker tottering by.

> ANN
> (*whispering discreetly*)
> Don't worry. She's the exception to the rule. Most everyone here is much more youthful.

EXT. GOLF COURSE – DAY

It is hot and sunny. Lenny is golfing alone, isolated.

Suddenly, from afar, he hears a woman's cries. He looks up.

Lenny's POV.

An older woman in a golfing outfit is running around, hysterical, calling for help. An older man, also in golf attire, lies motionless on the ground.

An ambulance arrives. Paramedics lift the older man on to a stretcher and take him away.

INT. DOCTOR'S OFFICE – DAY

Lenny sits across from the doctor.

> LENNY
> Are you sure?

> DOCTOR
> Look, you see this?
> (*illuminates an X-ray*)
> You're the picture of health.

> LENNY
> So no tumours.

> DOCTOR
> Nope.

> LENNY
> . . . And my heart?

DOCTOR

Like an ox. Lenny. You're gonna live to be a hundred.

LENNY

So I still have another thirty-five years.

DOCTOR
(*smiles*)

Just stay off the salt!

LENNY
(*musters a return smile*)

You bet!

EXT. LENNY AND MONA'S CONDO COMPLEX SWIMMING-POOL —
DAY

Lenny lies on a chaise-longue, alone by the poolside. Diane, perhaps slightly younger than Mona, approaches in high-heeled sandals.

DIANE

Hi, Lenny. Mind if I join you?

LENNY

No.

She arranges herself in a chair beside him. She lights up a cigarette, offers him one, he declines.

DIANE

So how's Mona?

LENNY

Fine.

DIANE

Inside on such a beautiful day?

LENNY

I dunno.

DIANE

What do you mean you don't know?

                    LENNY
I don't know.

                    DIANE
Whatever. So how are your girls doing?

                    LENNY
Fine, I guess.

                    DIANE
The grandchildren coming to visit soon?

                    LENNY
I dunno.

                    DIANE
Look, Lenny, I just think you ought to know: I heard about
you and Mona.

                    LENNY
What?

                    DIANE
About your getting divorced. I'm really sorry.

                    LENNY
We're not getting divorced.

                    DIANE
Divorced. Separated. Whatever. It doesn't matter. You're
alone now.

*Two beautiful young women come to the pool and settle themselves down
opposite. Lenny looks at them. He closes his eyes and turns away.*

                    DIANE
Anyway, if you ever need someone to talk to . . . you know
where to find me.

EXT. LENNY AND MONA'S CONDO VILLAGE ROADWAY – DAY

Mona is driving along.

INT. MONA'S CAR – DAY

Mona notices someone up ahead.

Mona's POV.

Of Diane jogging.

BACK TO:

Mona contemplating murder. She aims her car at Diane. But as she gets closer, a security guard suddenly appears. She waves with a friendly smile at Diane instead.

INT. HELEN'S PLACE – DAY

Intensity grips Helen as she ponders her book of poems, A Pornographic Childhood. *She rises, as if in pain, and starts pacing. She pounds a fist against her head.*

> HELEN
> (*voice-over*)
>
> Ugh . . . everything I write is so shallow, superficial. Can't anyone see through my work? Its inherent phoniness. 'Rape at Eleven', 'Rape at Twelve' . . . What the hell do I know about rape? I've never been raped. I'm just another sordid exploitationist. Oh . . . if only I'd been raped as a child! Then

10 Helen ponders the inanity of her poetry.

I would know authenticity! . . . But instead . . .
AGHHHHHH!

Finally she leaps onto her bed, thrashing about as if possessed.

                              HELEN
I'm no good! I'm no good! Nothing! Nothing! Zero! . . .

The telephone rings.

                              HELEN
Hello?

INT. ALLEN'S OFFICE – DAY

Allen is on the other end of the line. His breathing is heavy, low, constrained. He is sweating.

                              ALLEN
                      (*voice low and intense*)
I know who you are and you are nothing. You think you are fucking something, but you are fucking nothing. You are empty. You are a zero. You are a black hole, and I am going to fuck you so bad you're gonna be coming out of your ears.

Allen hangs up.

INT. HELEN'S PLACE – DAY

Helen presses ✲ 69.

BACK TO:

Allen at his desk, calming himself. The phone rings. He answers it.

                              ALLEN
Data Resources.

                              HELEN
                      (*voice-over*)
Who are you?

Allen hangs up. He is shaking, sweating profusely.

A pretty young secretary walks by outside his carrel and smiles. He smiles back, weakly.

11 Allen wonders whether he should ever have called Helen.

The phone rings again. Allen cannot resist answering it.

ALLEN

What do you want?

Pause.

HELEN
(*voice-over*)

I want you to fuck me.

Pause.

ALLEN

I . . . um . . . I don't think I can do that . . . I mean . . . I don't think I can do that.
> (*a beat; a co-worker is approaching*)

I gotta go.

HELEN
(*voice-over*)

Call me tomorrow.

ALLEN

. . . All right.

Allen hangs up. The co-worker appears.

CO-WORKER

Hey, Allen, did you see the play-offs last night?

ALLEN
(*smiling/joking*)

Yeah, pretty good! Pretty good!

CO-WORKER

I was on my knees praying for that shot!

ALLEN
(*laughs*)

It worked!

INT. ALLEN'S CAR – EVENING

Allen drinks and drives.

EXT. ALLEN AND HELEN'S APARTMENT BUILDING – LATER

Helen and her lover Jamal's silhouettes can be seen going at it next door to Allen.

INT. ALLEN'S PLACE – THAT MOMENT

Allen, drinking from a mostly empty liquor bottle, is studying a Playboy *centrefold. Faint but distinct sounds of Helen making love next door can be heard.*

The door buzzes.

> ALLEN

Who is it?

He puts down the magazine, rises unsteadily, and walks to the door.

> KRISTINA
> (*off-screen*)

It's uh . . . me. Kristina.

Allen opens the door.

> KRISTINA

Hey, how's it going?

> ALLEN

Okay.

> KRISTINA

Umm . . . I got some more info on Pedro.

> ALLEN

Pedro?

> KRISTINA

You know . . . the, uh –

> ALLEN

Oh, yeah. What?

> KRISTINA

Well, um . . .
> (*sees Allen tottering*)

Are you okay?

ALLEN

No.

KRISTINA

Here.

Kristina helps Allen back inside, sets him down on his bed.

ALLEN

. . . Pussy . . . Need pussy . . .

Allen passes out. Kristina falls on top of him.

She stares at him, pondering his face and body.

Finally, she takes off his glasses, leans her head against him, half lying down beside him.

Suddenly Allen awakens, rises, and rushes off to the bathroom. He throws up off-screen. Pause. When he reappears he sees Kristina on the bed.

ALLEN

What the fuck are you doing here?

Kristina is too petrified to speak.

ALLEN

Get out! Get out!!

Kristina leaves.

EXT. STREET – DAY

Joy walks along, despondent. Suddenly she hears a Russian-accented voice calling her. She looks around and sees a cab pulling up beside her. Vlad is inside.

VLAD

Joy! Joy! I am Vlad! Your student!

JOY

Oh, hello, Vlad. How are you?

VLAD

I am fine. How are you?

JOY

Oh, fine, fine.

Pause.

VLAD

I not believe you.

JOY

Really, Vlad. I'm fine!

Vlad sees Joy can no longer hold back her tears. He gets out of the cab.

JOY

I'm sorry. It's just . . . everyone hates me. I'm a terrible teacher. I should never have left telephone sales. I was doing more good then . . .

VLAD

Where you are go now?

JOY

Oh, I'm just on my way home.

VLAD

Tell me where do you live. I take you home.

JOY

Oh, no, I couldn't.

VLAD

Joy. Come in my car. I give you ride.

JOY

But I like walking. And the train is right nearby.

VLAD

No. No train. I drive you home.

JOY

But, Vlad. I live in New Jersey!

VLAD

Good. I take you New Jersey.

JOY

Maybe you don't understand. Vlad. New Jersey is far.

                              VLAD

Joy. You not understand. I driver. My taxi. You come. You
understand? You come.

Pause.

                              JOY

Are you sure you know . . .?

                              VLAD

Vlad know.

EXT. NEW JERSEY HIGHWAY – DAY

*'Joy's Happiness Theme' swells as Vlad's taxi speeds along. They pass a
'Welcome to New Jersey' sign.*

INT. HIGHWAY PIZZERIA – DAY

*Vlad and Joy are sitting in a booth, chewing a little meal in silence.
Finally:*

                              VLAD

I love New Jersey.

Pause.

                              JOY

Don't you miss Russia?

Pause.

                              VLAD

Fuck the cunt of Russia.

                              JOY

Well, I guess it's best to feel that way.

EXT. VLAD'S CAB – NIGHT

The taxi parks in front of Joy's house.

INT. VLAD'S CAB – NIGHT

Joy turns to Vlad.

JOY

Well, thank you for everything. That really was very nice of
you. I'm sorry about before . . . um . . . that was very unlike
me . . .

(*a beat*)

Do you think you'll need help finding your way back?

Vlad is silent. He stares off at her house, checks it out.

VLAD

Why you not married?

JOY

Oh, Vlad. Life is different in America. Here a woman can – I
know this is hard to understand – but a woman can fulfil her
potential. There are opportunities to do something, do good
. . . really improve the world . . .

VLAD

Do you like men?

12 Vlad asks Joy why she isn't married.

JOY
(*a beat*)
Yes . . . but . . . it's not so simple.

VLAD
Are you lesbian?

JOY
(*a beat*)
No.

VLAD
It's all right if you are lesbian. I like lesbian.

JOY
Vlad, I'm sorry. But this conversation has become a bit strange for me. Thank you for the ride, and . . . um . . .

Joy extends her hand for a handshake, but Vlad kisses her.

JOY
Oh. Well . . . then . . . good night and . . . uh . . . I'll see you –

But Vlad grabs her for another, longer kiss instead. Pause.

JOY
Would you like to come inside for a cup of tea?

INT. JOY'S ENTRANCEWAY – NIGHT

The door opens and Joy and Vlad come inside. Joy turns on the lights. An awkward pause.

JOY
I'll go turn on the kettle.

INT. JOY'S KITCHEN – NIGHT

Joy goes to the stove. Turning back she sees Vlad take off his shoes.

JOY
Oh . . . that's good . . . please take off your shoes. Make yourself comfortable.

INT. JOY'S LIVING-ROOM — NIGHT

Vlad wanders around, observing. Joy feels a little uncomfortable.

> JOY
>
> It's my parents' place. I plan on moving out soon, though.

> VLAD
>
> How long you live here?

> JOY
>
> Since I was born. But really, there are a lot of advantages to
> not moving.
> *(a beat)*
> So what did you do in Russia?

> VLAD
>
> I was thief.

> JOY
>
> Oh. Do you mean . . . the mafia?

> VLAD
>
> No. I am independent. I steal things on my own. Although I
> have many offers.
> *(sees Joy's guitar)*
> You are musician?

> JOY
>
> Oh, no, not really. I just write songs a little.

> VLAD
>
> What kind songs?

> JOY
>
> Oh, I don't know. They're all so terrible.

> VLAD
> *(a nod of understanding)*
> Love songs.
> *(a beat)*
> Play.
> *(Joy shakes her head, terrified)*
> I play.

Vlad begins playing and singing 'You Light up my Life'. He sings with intense emotion.

INT. JOY'S BEDROOM – LATER THAT NIGHT

Joy and Vlad finish making love to the song, 'You Light up my Life'.

>   VLAD
> . . . Okay.

>   JOY
>   (*a beat*)
> Okay?

>   VLAD
>   (*a beat*)
> I go now.

Vlad gets out of bed. Joy watches him gather his things, dress. Finally, as he disappears through the door:

>   JOY
> See you in class tomorrow!

EXT. ESL SCHOOL – DAY

The strikers pelt Joy with rubbish and epithets on her way inside, but she seems almost blissfully oblivious.

INT. CLASSROOM – DAY

Joy arrives filled with hope, but when she sees a nearly empty classroom, she can't help but be disappointed.

>   JOY
> Good morning.

A student arrives late, but it is not Vlad.

INT. TEACHERS' LOUNGE – DAY

Joy stares out the window, perhaps wistful, or melancholy. But then Rhonda joins her and she perks up.

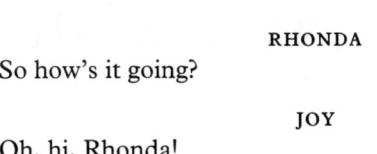

RHONDA

So how's it going?

JOY

Oh, hi, Rhonda!

RHONDA

Your students treating you okay?

JOY

Oh, they're just . . . great!

RHONDA

You know, I hate to have to say this, but: I told you so.

JOY

How about you? How's your class?

RHONDA

Oh, my students are such a hoot, always telling me how much
they love me. Actually . . . if you can keep a secret.
                    (*lowers her voice*)
There's this one Igor I've got such a crush on . . .

JOY

Oh?

RHONDA

Well, not that I'd ever . . . I mean, especially the Russians . . .

JOY

What?

Rhonda lifts her arm, points to her armpit, mouths 'b.o.'

JOY

Really? Mine seem okay . . .

RHONDA

Well, then, you're lucky.

JOY

Yeah. I guess I'm lucky.
                    (*a beat*)
Rhonda?

73

Yeah?

JOY

If your Igor . . .

RHONDA

. . . Used deodorant . . .

A Russian woman, Zhenia, suddenly interrupts, storming into the room. She stands before Joy looking very upset.

ZHENIA

You teacher Vlad?

JOY

Er . . . Yes.

Zhenia spits into Joy's face.

ZHENIA

Whore!

And she lunges for her, cursing in Russian. Rhonda and some other nearby teachers get her off Joy and out of the room.

RHONDA

Oh, my God! That woman was crazy! Joy, are you okay?

JOY
(*somewhat shaken*)

Yeah, I'm fine . . . Thank you . . .

A bell rings. Teachers et al. begin to disperse.

Joy gathers her stuff, Rhonda helping.

RHONDA
(*whispers*)

Joy, you didn't . . . did you?

Some teachers pause to overhear Joy's anticipated reply. But it doesn't come.

INT. JOHNNY'S BATHROOM – MORNING

Johnny stares into the toilet.

INT. JOHNNY'S PARENTS' BEDROOM – MORNING

He walks into his parents' bedroom. His mother, Betty Grasso, is
sleeping.

>   JOHNNY
> Mom?

>   BETTY
> Yeah?

>   JOHNNY
> There's blood in my b.m. Can I stay home from school
> today?

EXT. HOSPITAL – DAY

A 'National Children's Month' banner hangs outside across the
entrance.

INT. JOHNNY'S HOSPITAL ROOM – DAY

A detective is gently interrogating Johnny. Betty sits beside him. Joe
paces. A policeman stands by the door.

>   DETECTIVE
> How are you feeling?

>   JOHNNY
> Okay.

>   DETECTIVE
> You sure?

>   JOHNNY
> Yeah. I feel fine. Maybe a little sore. But I'm ready to go back
> to school.

>   DETECTIVE
> That's good! Now, Johnny. I have to ask you a few questions.
> Is that okay?

13 Johnny sees something wrong with his b.m.

JOHNNY

Yeah.

DETECTIVE

When did you first start feeling sick?

JOHNNY

Yesterday.

DETECTIVE

What happened?

JOHNNY

I threw up at my friend's house.

BETTY

Johnny spent the night there. I thought he just had a little virus.

DETECTIVE

Did you eat anything unusual?

JOHNNY

Just a tuna sandwich.

BETTY

He loves tuna salad.

DETECTIVE

I see. Johnny, when did you first notice the blood?

JOHNNY

When I went to the bathroom this morning.

DETECTIVE

Now, Johnny. I have to ask you a question. And it's very important that you be honest . . . Okay?

JOHNNY

Uh-huh.

DETECTIVE

Johnny, was there anyone in the last day or two . . . someone who . . . hurt you?

JOHNNY
(*a beat*)

No . . . I don't think so.

DETECTIVE

But someone did . . . hurt you. No, Johnny?

JOHNNY

No. No one hurt me.

JOE

Whadya mean no?! You've been fucking raped!!

A stunned silence. Joe hangs his head.

JOE

Sorry.

INT. MAPLEWOOD DINING-ROOM – EVENING

The family is at the dinner table.

TRISH

More potatoes, Bill?

BILL

Oh, no thanks. Mmm, I've got plenty.

TRISH

The babysitter should be here any minute now.

BILL

When does the PTA start?

TRISH

We've still got about half an hour.

BILL
(*to Billy*)

So how did school go today?

BILLY

Okay.

BILL

Was Johnny there?

BILLY

No.

TRISH

I sure hope you kids don't catch whatever he's got.

Timmy tries amusing everyone by pretending to throw up his potatoes.

TRISH

Very funny, Timmy. And now you are excused and can go right to bed.

TIMMY

But Mom –!

TRISH

Excuse me, Bill.

But then the phone rings. Trish lets go of Timmy, answers it.

TRISH

Hello? . . . Hi, Tawny . . . Yes, is there a problem? . . . Well, thank you for giving me so much notice . . . Yes, well, I'm sorry, too. You should have thought of that before . . . Goodbye.

Trish hangs up, returns to the table.

Bill, I'm sorry. You're going to have to go by yourself tonight.

BILL

Isn't there anyone else you can get?

TRISH

No, not at this late hour.

Trish sees the mess Timmy has been making with his potatoes and takes him away.

(*to Timmy*)
Now you can come with me and take a bath.

TIMMY

But I'm not finished!

TRISH

Come on! Let's go!

TIMMY

Wait! My Tamagotchi . . . my Tamagotchi!

Timmy grabs his Tamagotchi toy from the table as Trish hauls him upstairs.

Pause.

BILLY

Dad? If you and Mom died in a plane crash, would it be all right if I took over?

BILL

Well, probably one of your aunts would want to help out.

BILLY

So you don't think I'm old enough to take care of myself, Timmy and Chloe.

BILL

Well, no.

BILLY

Ronald Farber's parents are away in Europe for a few days, and Ronald gets to stay home alone by himself without a babysitter. Why do I need a babysitter?

BILL

Well, if you want to change Chloe's diapers . . .

BILLY

Well, if I didn't have any little brother or sister, would you let me stay alone by myself for a few days?

BILL

Your Mom and I are not Mr and Mrs Farber. We worry. So no.

BILLY

What if I were twelve?

BILL

No.

BILLY

Thirteen.

BILL
(*a beat*)
At thirteen, I think you'll be okay.

BILLY

Can you promise?

BILL
As long as you don't still look like you're eleven.

BILLY

I won't.

BILL
Okay. Thirteen, then.

INT. BILL'S CAR – NIGHT

Bill speaks on his car phone while driving.

BILL
Hello, in Roseland, please. I'm looking for the address of a
resident. The name is Farber . . . 11 Angel Court? . . . Thank
you.

He hangs up.

EXT. ROAD – NIGHT

Bill's car turns on to Angel Court, disappearing off into the night.

FADE TO BLACK.

INT. MAPLEWOOD KITCHEN – NIGHT

*Bill takes a half-gallon of milk out of a plastic bag and puts it in the
refrigerator.*

TRISH
(*off-screen*)
Hon, is that you?

                              BILL
        Yeah.

                              TRISH
                           (off-screen)
        You remember the milk?

                              BILL
        Yeah.

INT. MAPLEWOOD TV ROOM – NIGHT

Bill walks by the TV room where Trish is sitting watching TV alone.

                              TRISH
        How was the meeting?

                              BILL
        It was fine.

                              TRISH
        Bill, are you all right?

                              BILL
        I think I have to lie down.

                              TRISH
        Oh, shit. I hope you're not coming down with whatever that
        Johnny Grasso had.

                              BILL
        I don't think so.

He walks off.

INT. MAPLEWOOD FOYER – NIGHT

Bill walks up the stairs in a daze.

                              TRISH
                           (off-screen)
        Be up in a minute!

INT. BILLY'S ROOM – NIGHT

Bill stops by Billy's bed. Back issues of Kool *magazine lie piled on the floor.*

Billy is asleep. A Playboy *magazine sticks out from beneath his pillow.*

Bill goes over to Billy and bends down. He kisses him.

> BILLY

Dad?

> BILL

Yeah?

> BILLY

I . . . I . . . I almost came.

Billy closes his eyes again.

INT. BILL AND TRISH'S BEDROOM – LATER THAT NIGHT

Lights out. Bill lies awake, listening to Trish's rhythmic breathing.

> BILL

Trish? . . . Trish?

> TRISH

. . . Mmmyeah?

Pause.

> BILL

Do you love me?

> TRISH

Oh, Bill . . . Yes.

> BILL

No, I mean, do you really love me? No matter what.

> TRISH

No matter what . . . what?

> BILL

No matter . . . whatever . . .

TRISH

Bill. You have me. You always will.

A long pause.

BILL

I'm sick . . .

TRISH
(*barely awake*)
Aww . . . Take some Tylenol. You'll feel better tomorrow.

Bill turns away.

INT. LENNY AND MONA'S CONDO – NIGHT

Lenny and Mona are preparing for bed, watching TV.

MONA

I met with Steven Zimmer this morning.

LENNY

You like him?

MONA

Yeah. I'm gonna hire him.

LENNY

Good. I'm gonna use Marty Blau.

MONA

Good. I feel so much better now.

LENNY

Well, good. It shouldn't take too long. Good night.

Pause.

MONA

Lenny?

LENNY

Yeah?

MONA

Can you sleep on the couch?

84

LENNY

Why?

MONA

Steven Zimmer thought it would be a good idea.

Pause.

LENNY

Okay.

Lenny gets out of bed and leaves the room.

INT. DIANE'S PLACE – DAY

Lenny follows Diane into her spacious abode. She fixes a couple of drinks, turns on a CD.

DIANE

Gin and tonic?

LENNY

Okay. Thanks.

14 Diane fixes a drink.

85

DIANE

Uch, it's so bright outside. It gives me a headache just looking out that window.

LENNY

Yeah, well, they say it's gonna rain tomorrow.

DIANE

I don't want to talk about the fucking weather.

LENNY

Well, it's good for playing golf.

DIANE

I hate that game. It's so boring.

LENNY

It passes the time.

DIANE

I like to travel.

LENNY

I went to Europe once.

DIANE

You ever been to Tahiti? How about Tunisia? A night in Tunisia? Vincent never liked to travel.

LENNY

I guess I'm like Vincent.

DIANE

You know when I was a child I always imagined I'd marry the man I fell in love with, have a son and a daughter who loved me as much as I hated my mother. Then die . . . tragically and suddenly, young and beautiful. When Vincent left me I imagined I'd finally be happy.

LENNY

I guess you haven't lost your imagination.

DIANE

Lenny, I gotta get outta here. I can't breathe. All the women are pathetic gossips and the men are just . . .

LENNY

. . . pathetic?

DIANE

I don't want to die here.

LENNY

You just don't want to die.

DIANE

Not alone.

They make love. Afterwards, Lenny turns away.

DIANE

Don't. Don't feel guilty.

LENNY

I don't. I don't feel anything.

INT. ALLEN'S PLACE – EVENING

Allen sits on his bed, tense and sweaty, gripping his phone.

INT. HELEN'S PLACE – EVENING

Helen lies on her bed, strewn with poetry books and papers, concentrating on her phone.

The phone rings. She answers it. She hears only some faint breathing. For a while she says nothing.

BACK TO:

Allen on the phone with Helen, saying nothing. Finally:

HELEN
(*voice-over*)

I have to meet you.

Allen hangs up and unplugs the phone. Pause.

The door buzzes. Allen rises, walks to the door.

ALLEN

Who is it?

KRISTINA
(*off-screen*)

It's me . . . Kristina.

Allen hesitates, then opens the door. Pause.

I'm sorry about last night.

ALLEN

Yeah . . . uh . . . me too. I shouldn't have . . . um . . .

KRISTINA

I understand. I mean . . . See, I can admit it. That I'm fat and ugly.

ALLEN

No, no . . .

KRISTINA

Yes, yes . . .

Tears are trickling down Kristina's face. Allen hands her a crumpled (i.e. used) tissue.

Thank you.

Pause.

ALLEN

Say, you wanna go somewhere?

Kristina nods, grateful.

EXT. BAR – NIGHT

Music flows outside.

INT. BAR – NIGHT

Allen and Kristina slow-dance by the jukebox.

INT. COFFEE SHOP – NIGHT

Allen and Kristina sit in a booth. They have finished eating.

15 Allen and Kristina dance.

ALLEN

I like you.

Pause.

KRISTINA

I have a confession to make.

ALLEN

Oh?

KRISTINA

Remember Pedro's penis?

ALLEN

You mean, the one that was . . . cut off?

KRISTINA

Yeah . . . well, it wasn't really cut off.

ALLEN

What happened to it?

                              KRISTINA
                             (*a beat*)
Nothing.

                              ALLEN
I – I don't understand. Umm . . . Why would you make
something like that up?
                           (*no response*)
Was Pedro even killed?

Kristina nods.

How do you . . .?

Pause.

                              KRISTINA
I tried so many times to tell you – but it's hard to –
                             (*a beat*)
I'd always been very friendly to him. I try to be that way with
all the doormen, even though they're usually snickering
behind my back. I don't care, I'm still friendly. It's my way.
But Pedro was different. Pedro never snickered. Of course,
who was he to snicker? He wasn't exactly Tom Cruise. Still,
he could have, and he didn't. So anyway, one night . . .

INT. ALLEN AND HELEN'S APARTMENT LOBBY – NIGHT

Pedro opens the door for Kristina.

                              KRISTINA
                           (*voice-over*)
. . . I was coming home from the twenty-four hour Pathmark
. . . It was late . . .

                              PEDRO
Good evening.

                              KRISTINA
Hi, Pedro. Do you think you could help me with these bags?

                              PEDRO
No problem.

Pedro locks up and takes the bags from Kristina. They then walk to the elevator.

> KRISTINA
> (*voice-over*)
> Normally I don't need any help, but my back hurt because the bags were heavy. And I had a half-gallon of strawberry ice-cream, two boxes of fudge, and a key lime pie . . . Really, I just couldn't wait to snuggle up under the covers and watch TV. You know . . .

INT. ELEVATOR — NIGHT

Kristina and Pedro stand waiting for the elevator to reach her floor.

> KRISTINA
> (*voice-over*)
> It was in the elevator that I first got a funny feeling . . . like he was looking at me kind of funny . . . but I thought maybe he was just being friendly too . . . I mean, you know, just two friendly people.

INT. HALLWAY — NIGHT

Kristina and Pedro get off and walk to her apartment. She takes out her keys.

INT. KRISTINA'S PLACE — NIGHT

Pedro follows Kristina inside, brings the groceries into the kitchen.

> KRISTINA
> Well, thank you so much, Pedro.

> PEDRO
> No problem.

There is an awkward pause. Kristina realizes that she hasn't tipped him.

> KRISTINA
> Oh, I'm so sorry.

PEDRO

Forget about that. What I'd really like is a scoop of your ice-cream before I go back down.

KRISTINA

Oh, sure . . . please have a seat.

Kristina begins to scoop some ice-cream.

PEDRO

My wife died three years ago . . . I feel so lonely . . .
(rising)
You are a beautiful woman, Kristina . . . you are so beautiful . . .

Pedro grabs her and forces her to kiss him. Kristina screams.

BACK TO:

Allen and Kristina in the coffee shop.

KRISTINA

. . . and next thing I knew he was . . . inside me, just pounding away. Oh, Allen!

Kristina cries into her napkin. Pause.

The waitress comes by.

WAITRESS

All finished?

ALLEN

Yeah.

KRISTINA

I guess so.

WAITRESS

Would you like to see a dessert menu?

KRISTINA

What kind of ice-cream do you have?

WAITRESS

Chocolate, vanilla and strawberry.

KRISTINA

Okay. Then I'll just have a plain chocolate fudge sundae with
strawberry ice-cream. Thank you.

WAITRESS

And you, sir?

ALLEN

Just the check, please.

The waitress leaves.

KRISTINA

So anyway, everything got really quiet and I thought, okay,
well, at least the worst is over . . .

INT. KRISTINA'S PLACE – NIGHT

Pedro lies on top of Kristina

PEDRO

How do you like it?

KRISTINA

Kiss me again.
                    (*voice-over*)
But, that was just an act. I let him kiss me one last time, and
then . . . grabbed a hold of his neck and . . . twisted it . . .

Kristina breaks Pedro's neck.

BACK TO:

Allen and Kristina in the coffee shop.

KRISTINA

. . . backward.

The waitress comes by with the dessert and the check.

WAITRESS

Here you are.

KRISTINA

Thank you.
                    (*while eating her sundae*)

And then I had to cut up his body, plastic-bag all the parts
. . . I've been throwing it out gradually ever since. There's
still some left in my freezer.

Pause.

ALLEN
So you did cut off his . . .

KRISTINA
No. I left it attached. I didn't want to have to touch it again.
                    (*a beat; then sobbing*)
I feel so terrible. You must think I'm a monster. But what else
could I have done? . . . Anyway, I couldn't help myself. I hate
. . . sex. I'm sorry, but just the idea of it . . . of someone all
over . . . inside . . . me . . . I know it isn't right, but . . . Can
we still be . . . friends?

ALLEN
Um . . . I guess . . . Yeah . . . I mean, we all have our . . .
you know . . . our pluses and minuses . . .

Pause.

KRISTINA
It was a crime of passion.
                    (*a beat*)
I'm a passionate woman.

FADE TO BLACK.

INT. ALLEN'S PLACE – NIGHT

*Allen stares at his telephone. Finally, he plugs it in. Instantly it rings.
He answers it.*

HELEN
(*voice-over*)
I've had you on auto-redial all night.

Allen hangs up and unplugs the phone again.

INT. APARTMENT HALLWAY – NIGHT

Allen comes out of his apartment and walks bravely down towards

Helen's apartment. He stops outside her door. Pause. He buzzes.
A moment passes. Allen covers the peephole with his hand.

> HELEN
> (*off-screen*)

Hello?

Helen opens the door, sees Allen.

> HELEN

Yes?

Pause.

> ALLEN

I'm the . . . um . . .

> HELEN

I'm sorry?
> (*a beat*)

Oh.

She cannot disguise her disappointment, but tries.

> HELEN

Come in.

> ALLEN

Okay.

INT. HELEN'S PLACE – NIGHT

Helen and Allen sit opposite each other. A long silence. Finally:

> HELEN

Please have a seat. Drink?

> ALLEN

No . . . thanks.

Pause.

> HELEN

This isn't working.

16 Allen tries reaching out to Helen.

> ALLEN

No.

> HELEN

You're not my type.

> ALLEN

No.

INT. APARTMENT HALLWAY – NIGHT

Allen walks back towards his door, pauses, looks at the other side of the hallway: he decides to go visit Kristina instead.

He buzzes Kristina's door.

After a few moments, the door opens. Allen looks at the ground.

> ALLEN

Can I come in?

INT. KRISTINA'S PLACE – NIGHT

Allen and Kristina prepare for bed. They look at each other, pause, then lie down side by side, but facing opposite directions.

17 Allen decides to visit Kristina.

INT. SUBWAY TRAIN – DAY

Joy sits on the train. She is carrying a bouquet of flowers.

INT. SEEDY BUILDING – DAY

Joy climbs a few flights of stairs, arrives at a door with the number 8D on it. She buzzes, then waits. She hears quarrelling, in Russian.

Zhenia opens the door. She has a black eye and a cut lip.

> JOY
>
> Oh . . . er . . . I'm sorry . . . I just wanted to . . . er . . . Here . . .

Joy shoves her bouquet of flowers into Zhenia's hand. She is about to beat a hasty retreat when Zhenia suddenly calls:

> ZHENIA
>
> Vlad!

Zhenia abandons Joy at the door and goes back inside, muttering obscenities (in Russian).

Vlad appears at the door, surprised to see her. Oddly, Joy seems equally surprised to see him.

> VLAD

Come inside.

INT. VLAD AND ZHENIA'S PLACE – DAY

Joy follows Vlad inside. He motions for her to sit. She notices her guitar and CD player lying against the far wall.

> VLAD

Please.

Vlad sits down opposite her. Zhenia brings in a cup of tea. Zhenia's mother sniffles and shuffles about in the background.

> JOY
> (*to Zhenia*)

Spaceebo.

Vlad signals Zhenia to scram.

> VLAD

Joy. Why you are come here?

> JOY

I came because I wanted to say that I was sorry to your wife.

> VLAD

Zhenia is not my wife.

> JOY

So you're really not married?

Pause.

> VLAD

Zhenia love me. It is problem. She want be my wife, but she don't listen. What can I do? What can I do?
> (*a beat*)
Come. You want I drive you New Jersey? We go shopping mall?

No, thank you. I don't think that's really . . .

There is a crash, and a baby starts crying off-screen. Vlad and Zhenia start shouting at each other.

When things cool down Zhenia returns with a tray of pastries and vodka.

VLAD

Joy. I must ask you question.

JOY

Yes?

VLAD

But I very ashamed.

JOY

I'm sure I'll understand.

VLAD

Good. Can I borrow money? It is very important.

18 Vlad asks Joy for money.

Pause.

Joy glances over at Zhenia standing at the other end of the room. Zhenia's face is anxious, pleading.

JOY

How much?

VLAD

One thousand dollars.

JOY

A th – thou –

VLAD

All right. Five hundred. I need money now.

JOY

Well, I guess I could go to a cash machine . . .

VLAD

Good. I know where is ATM.

Vlad rises quickly. Joy hesitates.

JOY

Vlad?

VLAD

Yes?

JOY

Could I first have my guitar and my CD player back?

VLAD
(considers her proposal, then:)
Okay. It is deal.

EXT. STREET IN BRIGHTON BEACH – EVENING

Joy and Vlad emerge from a bank.

VLAD

Do you think shopping mall in New Jersey is open tonight?

JOY

Yeah. Probably.
> (*hands Vlad the money*)

Here.

VLAD
> (*embraces Joy*)

Joy. I love you.

JOY

You love New Jersey.

VLAD

I give you back Monday.

JOY
> (*taking back her guitar from Vlad*)

That's okay. Uh . . . I probably won't be there anyway.

VLAD

Why no?

JOY

I don't know, I think . . . now I have more sympathy for the strikers.
> (*a beat*)

See ya.

Vlad watches Joy walk away with her guitar.

VLAD
> (*muttering to himself*)

Stupid American.

And he walks off in the opposite direction.

INT. MAPLEWOOD DINING-ROOM – EVENING

The family is at the table, eating dinner.

BILL

So, Billy, how was school today?

BILLY

Okay. Ronald Farber was absent.

BILL

Oh?

BILLY

He was afraid of the math test.

TRISH

So he stayed home?

BILLY

Yeah. He cut.

TRISH

Oh, that's terrible. His parents . . .

BILLY

They don't know yet. They're still on vacation.

TRISH

Oh, are they gonna be upset.

BILLY

Well, Ronald's gonna be pretty upset when he finds out the test was cancelled.

BILL

What happened?

BILLY

Mrs Paley was absent also.

TRISH
(*chuckles*)

Oh, gee!

BILL

Did you call Ronald and tell him?

BILLY

Yeah, but there was no answer.

TRISH

So was Mrs Paley sick, then?

BILLY

Well, everyone said she was just too strung out.

TRISH

Now why do people say things like that?

BILLY

Because she's a drug addict.

TRISH

And how do you know?

BILLY

Mom. Everyone knows.

TRISH

Well, I didn't know. Did you know, Bill?

BILL

No.

BILLY

Well, it's what everyone says: she's a junkie. And she's
probably gonna get fired. It's really sad.

TRISH

Well, if Mrs Paley turns out, in fact, to be a junkie, then she
should be fired. Don't you think so, Bill?

BILL

I don't know. Don't you think that's a little harsh? I mean, if
it's not affecting her work . . .

TRISH

Well, apparently it is. And no, in fact, I don't think it's a little
harsh at all. I'm sorry, but when it comes to drug abuse . . .
and children, my children . . . Uch, they should all just be
locked up and throw away the key. And Billy, I want you to
know, if you ever even think of doing drugs, and end up dying
in a hospital . . . I'd disown you. That's how strongly I feel.

BILL

Trish . . .

TRISH

Now I know, Bill, I may sound harsh, but we're talking about
our kids. Not to be too grandiose, but this is the future, the
future of our country we're talking about, after all.

A pause. The telephone rings.

TRISH

I'll get it.
> (*answers the phone*)

Hello, who's calling, please? . . . Oh, hi . . . Sure, hold on . . .
> (*to Bill*)

It's Joe Grasso.

BILL

Oh, great! Thanks!
> (*rises, picks up the phone*)

Hey, Joe! What's up? How's Johnny doing?

JOE
> (*voice-over*)

You're a dead man.

Bill hears the click of Joe hanging up.

BILL
> (*fakes continuing the conversation*)

Oh, good, good . . . No problem! . . . Right . . . Okay. Well,
take care . . . Bye!

TRISH

How's Johnny doing?

BILL

Oh, fine, fine! Never better!

TRISH

Good. 'Cause we bought those *Beauty and the Beast* tickets for
this Saturday and I don't think Billy has anyone else . . .

BILL

No, no . . . he didn't cancel . . .

The doorbell rings.

TRISH

Now who could that be?

BILL

I'll get it.

INT. MAPLEWOOD FOYER – EVENING

Bill goes to the front door.

> BILL

Who is it?

> VOICE

Police.

Bill opens the door. The detective seen earlier at the hospital is there with a police officer.

> BILL

Can I help you?

> DETECTIVE

Are you William Maplewood?

> BILL

Yes.

> DETECTIVE

We're sorry to disturb you, but we have some questions for you and your wife. It has to do with your son's friend, Johnny Grasso.

> BILL

Did something . . . ?
> *(a meaningful silence)*
Come this way.

Bill escorts them into the living-room.

> BILL

Sit . . . please.

> TRISH
> *(off-screen)*

Bill, who is it?

> BILL

We're just finishing dinner, but I – I'll be right back.

Bill hurries back to the dining-room.

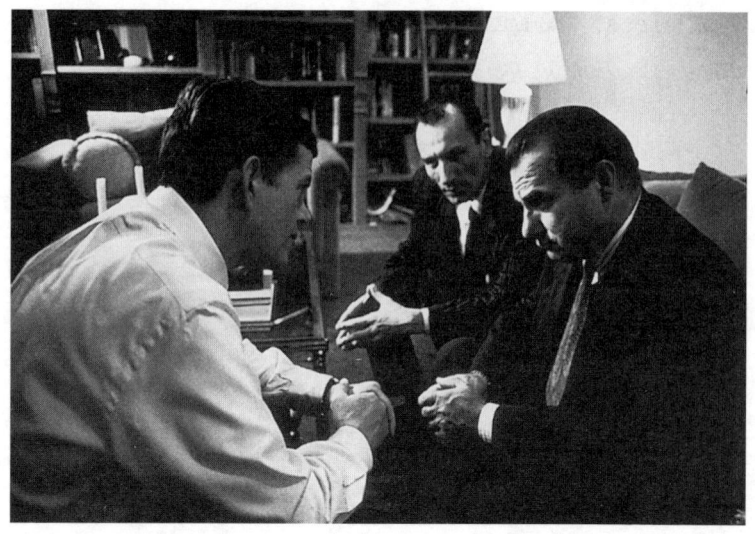

19 The detective has a few questions for Bill.

> BILL
> (*mouths to Trish*)

The police.

> (*a beat*)

You take care of the kids.

Bill returns to his guests in the living-room. He is noticeably jittery.

> BILL

Sorry. Now . . . you said something about Ronald Farber?

> DETECTIVE

Excuse me?

The detective is nonplussed.

> BILL

I'm sorry . . . er . . . I mean . . . I mean, Johnny Grasso?

EXT. MAPLEWOOD HOME – MORNING

Holding Timmy's hand, Trish comes rushing out the front door in her robe and slippers.

A schoolbus is waiting at the corner.

> TIMMY

I wanna stay home . . .

> TRISH
> (*calling to the bus*)

One second!
> (*calling inside*)

Hurry up, Billy! The bus is here! Wait!!!

Billy hurries on out, but the bus has already taken off.

All right, I'll take you boys myself.

Defeated, Trish, Billy and Timmy turn back to the house, then suddenly stop and look: the words 'Serial Rapist' and 'Pervert' have been spray-painted on to their housefront.

INT. MAPLEWOOD HOME – EVENING

The family eats at the dinner table. No one talks. The mood is tense.

INT. MAPLEWOOD TV ROOM – NIGHT

Bill is sitting on the couch, looking disconsolate, when Billy appears. He sits down beside his father.

> BILLY

Dad?

> BILL

Yes, Billy?

> BILLY

Everyone at school is saying things about you.

> BILL

Who is everyone?

> BILLY

Kids. You know. Everyone.

> BILL

What are they saying?

Pause.

                              BILLY

That you're a serial rapist.

                              BILL

Oh.

                              BILLY

And a pervert.

                              BILL

You mean, like what they painted on the house.

Billy nods. Pause.

                              BILLY

Dad . . . did you . . . did you . . . um . . . with Johnny Grasso
and Ronald Farber . . .?

Pause.

                              BILL

Yes.

Pause.

                              BILLY

What did you . . . do?

                              BILL

I . . . I touched them . . .

                              BILLY

Whadya mean exactly . . . touched . . .?

                              BILL

I . . . fondled them.

Pause.

                              BILLY

What for?

                              BILL

I couldn't help myself.

Pause.

> **BILLY**
>
> What else?

> **BILL**
>
> I unzipped myself . . .

> **BILLY**
>
> You mean . . . masturbated?

> **BILL**
>
> No.

> **BILLY**
>
> Then . . . what?

> **BILL**
>
> I . . . made love . . .

Pause.

> **BILLY**
>
> What do you . . . mean?

> **BILL**
>
> I fucked them.

Pause.

> **BILLY**
>
> What was it like?

> **BILL**
>
> It was . . . great.

Pause.

> **BILLY**
>
> Would you do it again?

> **BILL**
>
> Yes.

Pause.

> BILLY

Would you ever fuck me?

> BILL

No . . . I jerk off instead.

Bill weeps, while Billy sobs uncontrollably.

EXT. MAPLEWOOD HOME – DAYBREAK

Trish carries Chloe and a suitcase as she rushes Billy and Timmy out to the car. Kooki follows along.

> TIMMY

Mommy, I'm tired. I don't wanna go. I want my Tamagotchi!

> TRISH

Shh! Quiet! It's okay, I've got your Tamagotchi.

They get in the hastily packed car and drive off.

FADE TO BLACK.

A TITLE CARD READS: SIX MONTHS LATER

CUT TO:

EXT. MONA'S CONDO TERRACE – DAY

Billy stands on the terrace and looks down. He sees palm trees. He sees the ocean. He sees a beautiful woman sunbathing by the pool. Talk of turkey and weather filters out to him.

Kooki stands beside him.

INT. MONA'S NEW CONDOMINIUM – DAY

Lenny, Mona, Trish, Helen and Joy sit at a long table filled with holiday food. Timmy watches TV off-screen. Chloe sleeps in her crib off-screen.

> TRISH

So who used to live here before?

> MONA

Another couple . . . the Hellers.

20 Billy and Kooki take in the view from Mona's new condo.

What happened to them?

MONA

They got divorced.

Pause.

HELEN

. . . Anyway, so the police came and looked in her freezer and found baggies filled with the doorman's genitals.

Pause. Lenny salts his food, a heavy dose.

MONA

I use baggies.

JOY

Me too.

HELEN

Everyone uses baggies. That's why we can all relate to the crime. Don't you see?

TRISH

I can't relate to it.

Pause.

HELEN

. . . In any case, there's this guy I've met, Joy, that I think you'd like. He's into computers, I think.

JOY

How did you meet him?

HELEN

He's a neighbour of mine. Do you wanna call him, or should I give him your number?

JOY

I'll call him.

HELEN

That would be great. I think he'd really like that.

TRISH

What about me?

HELEN

I'm looking. I'm looking.

TRISH

I like computers.

HELEN

Trish, trust me on this one: not for you.

MONA

And what about me?

HELEN

I haven't forgotten, Mom. It's just it's hard. But I'm looking
for everyone.

LENNY

Don't look for me.

HELEN

Have you found someone?

LENNY

No. There is no one.

Pause.

MONA

I heard Diane had a stroke.

LENNY

She'll recover.

MONA

That's good.

JOY

Where there's life there's hope.

TRISH

That's right.

HELEN

You bet.

MONA

Absolutely.

LENNY

Yeah.

Pause.

JOY

Could you pass over the sweet potatoes, please?

TRISH

Sure.

Pause. Lenny resalts his food.

Did anyone watch Leno last night?

Everyone shakes his head or mumbles no.

Timmy walks by, dejected.

MONA

Timmy, Timmy . . . Come over and sit on Grandma's lap
. . . Timmy?

Timmy ignores her, picks up his toy laser gun, returns to the TV room.

JOY

What's the matter with Timmy?

TRISH

His Tamagotchi died.

Pause.

MONA

So what's going to happen now to that woman who killed
your doorman?

HELEN

I don't know, Mom. But it's so sad. She's all alone.
(*a beat*)

I wish I'd gotten to know her better. We might have found we had something in common.

> JOY

Maybe you'll write a poem about her.

Helen bursts out laughing.

> HELEN

Oh, Joy, I'm sorry. But don't worry. I'm not laughing at you. I'm laughing with you.

> JOY

But I'm not laughing.

EXT. MONA'S CONDO TERRACE — DAY

Close on Billy as his face expresses growing intensity.

Billy's POV of the beautiful woman sunbathing down by the pool. She unhooks her bikini top.

BACK TO:

Billy climaxing.

Close on Kooki licking up Billy's little puddle of sperm on the railing.

INT. MONA'S NEW CONDO — DAY

The meal is painfully silent. Finally:

> MONA

Let's make a toast.

> JOY

To happiness.

> EVERYONE ELSE

To happiness!

Glasses clink. Some hesitation before everyone downs the wine. Laughter. Kooki races in, jumps into Trish's lap, licks her face.

> TRISH

Kooki!

Billy enters. He is ecstatic. Tears well up in his eyes.

BILLY

I came!

CUT TO BLACK.